LOVE

LEAMON WHITE

Published 2024

Printed in the United States of America

First Edition

ISBN (softcover): 978-1-963380-84-2
ISBN (e-book): 978-1-963380-85-9

For information, address:

Holzer Books LLC
8 The Green, Ste. A
Dover, Delaware 19901 USA

For information about special discounts available for bulk purchases, sales promotions, and educational needs, contact:

info@holzerbooksllc.com
+1 (888) 901-7776

holzerbooksLLC©

CONTENTS

THE ONE THE LORD GAVE TO ME

I had a personal conversation with the LORD

the other night and I told HIM about some of the

things that I've been going through in my life.

Some of them made me happy and some made me sad.

Then HE said to me, *those things that you went through,*

were just tests to see how you would handle them.

HE also said to me, *sometimes you have to go through*

the fire in order to get to your happy place in life.

Not only that, HE then said to me, *I knew you were going to*

go through those things before you were even born.

HE then said, *because you have been so good and steadfast, I*

decided to give you the greatest gift of all

and that gift will be the most beautiful and precious gift

I will ever give to you.

Your beautiful mate!

Have a happy life.

From, LORD

WHEN YOU'RE LOVED

You know you're loved

when you wake up in the morning.

You know you're loved

when you've done all you can do on earth.

You know you're loved

when you lay your head down for the last time

and GOD says, "Job well done, my child."

you can come home now."

WHEN

When I think about you,

I thank God.

When I dream about you,

I thank God.

When I know you're coming,

I thank God.

When I see you,

I thank God.

When I hold you,

I thank God.

LOVE

When I feel your heart beat,
I thank God.

When I kiss you,
I thank God.

When I hear your voice,
I thank God.

When I hear your laugh,
I thank God.

When I watch you do all
that you do,
I thank God.

When I watch you as
you sleep at night,
I thank God.

When I caress your
beautiful silky skin

LEAMON WHITE

I thank God.

When we have those
special moments that
will last for eternity,
I thank God.

I praise and thank God for
given to me, the greatest
gift of love I'll ever receive
in this life, you.

THE TWELFTH ROSE

The first rose means,

from the day we first met,

I had beautiful dreams of you and I

and the desire to make them all come true.

The second rose means,

I will turn on the flames of passion

in the deepest darkest corridors of your heart

that have been dormant for so long,

not only giving them light,

but giving them life once again.

The third rose means,

I will give to you my love,

the affection of all that I am, and

I will care for you with the passion

a mother has for her child, forever.

The fourth rose means,

I will care for you the one I love,

with all that I am.

Never asking for anything in return,

except to say,

I will always be there for you.

The fifth rose means,

I will protect your life

for the precious jewel that it is,

and caress it with my heart and soul,

with every ounce of love I have and beyond.

The sixth rose means,

I will be devoted to you and only you,

giving all that I am exclusively to you,

and to none other as long as we live.

The seventh rose means,

I will always be as close as the rhythms

of your heart,

for when your spirit is low from the oppressions of life,

so on those times you can't call,

all you need do, is listen.

The eighth rose means,

I will place you on a pedestal on high,

above all the rest who aren't worthy in my eyes

to walk this life with me as my companion.

The ninth rose means,

I will romance you for all eternity,

for you are the apple of my eye,

the center of all my thoughts,

and not only the nucleus of my heart,

but the beat itself.

The tenth rose means,

I will cherish every moment with the sensitivity of the first,

and the sparks will remain throughout

all eternity.

The eleventh rose means,

I will love you with every ounce of my

being, for all I am worth, with all my heart,

body and soul, and if that is not enough, I'll

love you even more.

The twelfth rose is the most special of all.

For without the twelfth rose,

all is not complete.

You see, the twelfth rose,

is the summation of the first eleven,

and all that I am.

It means,

I will give to you the one I love

the essence of all my being,

the very fibers of my heart and soul,

and the most precious gift of all,

LOVE.

So let it be known, that this

is my personal declaration to you,

LOVE

I love you and only you very much,

and I will always be your, Twelfth Rose.

Love

is a disease

that you should

try to catch

on purpose.

It feels

good, cuddly,

warm and cozy.

So catch it.

Then give it

to someone else.

A MESSAGE TO MY MOTHER

When I was first conceived, you and the LORD were the only ones who knew. While I was in my watery cocoon world you nurtured and took care of me. When I made my grand entrance into this vast unknown place we so affectionately call Mother Earth, you protected me with your life and wisdom. So it's no wonder I feel about you the way I do.

So I thought I'd drop you a message about a personal conversation I had with the LORD. I gave the LORD a call one night and when HE answered I told HIM the following:

"I know when I die, I will be present with YOU." I also explained to HIM, that if HE would have me come back to Earth to complete a task left undone, I want the same mother I had the first time, the second time around. With that said, I then reminded HIM of the fact that HE has never made a mistake throughout all eternity.

The LORD then replied, *"My precious child, I love you and I would never have it any other way. I too, have a mother and if I had it to do all over again, your request of me, would be my request to my father. Like you, my child, I love my mother just as you love yours."*

The LORD then said, *"Consider your request granted. Besides, you can't replace, **PERFECTION**."*

You

If I were the

Only one on Earth,

All by myself,

No one else around,

Just me,

Only me,

Somehow,

Someway,

I would still find,

You!

Falling In Love

Falling in love is a big step in life. It means, you have found that special someone you are willing to walk this life with hand in hand.

However, there are some things you need to learn about when you are ready to take that walk of life with someone.

When you are ready to take that walk with someone, don't just listen to the words coming out of their mouth, knock on the door of their heart and when it opens, walk in and conduct a thorough analyzation of the interior of their heart. You will learn some interesting things about that person.

When you walk in look at the walls of the heart and see the pictures of the past. This will help you to understand them better and help you see your future with that person.

Then look at all the cracks inside. This will tell you about the pain, hurt, suffering and disappointments and will help you learn how to navigate around and get rid of the pain, soften the hurt, and eliminate the suffering and forever get rid of all disappointments so your life will be at peace.

Once you have conducted your investigation, there is one last thing you must do. Exit the heart and come back outside. Close the door and then look into the eyes of the one you love and see your future together and start your walk in life. This way you will surly know what your life walk will be like and all the happiness and joy will be. There is an old saying, *"The Eyes Have It"* and so will you. Now you can start your walk together.

Things You Need To Know

When you said,

"I Love You,"

you made me happy.

When you said,

"I want to walk this life with you,"

you made me the happiest person

ever created.

I Love You!

You are the best present

I ever received in my life.

I Love You!

Dating you was a dream come true.

LOVE

When we became one, it was then I knew our hearts beat the

same rhythm.

I Love You!

I love the way your sexy

drives me crazy.

I Love You!

Seeing you turns me on.

Touching you sets me on fire.

Holding you makes me explode

with love for you.

I Love You!

A kiss from you is better

medicine then any hospital

injection could ever be.

I Love You!

Kissing you up one side and

down the other drives me crazy.

I Love You!

When I have to set the timing on

my watch, I just watch you walk

and that let's me know the timing

is perfect.

I Love You!

Your touch is like a magic

wand. When you touch me, all

my worries just disappear.

I Love You!

Whether it's morning, noon, evening

or night, the essence of your beauty

is intoxicating and sexy to me.

I Love You!

All my hopes, wishes and dreams

meant nothing until I met you.

It was then I realized, they were

meant to be shared with someone

special, you.

LOVE

I Love You!

Whether you hold my hand, give me

a hug, give me a kiss or stare into

my eyes, my body get's warm all

over and I know I'm loved.

I Love You!

My life is incomplete

without you in it.

I Love You!

It's not the way you look at me

it's the thought behind the look

that turns me on and

and sets me on fire.

I Love You!

I have a lot to give

and only want to give

it to you.

I Love You!

I didn't know what beautiful, sexy and gorgeous really meant,

until you came into my life.

I Love You!

My world is a better

place now that you're in it.

I Love You!

It feels so good to love you

and you love me back the

same way.

It makes my heart sing.

I Love You!

You are the beat of my heart,

the blood in my veins

and my reason for living. Wow, what a life!

I Love You!

I didn't know how to

spell sexy, beautiful, gorgeous, lovely, wonderful, kind hearted, caring, helpful, nurturing or any words the like,

until I met you.

I Love You!

Everything in my life means nothing if you're not in my life

to share it with me.

I Love You!

You don't batteries.

You have me. I'm

24/7 ready and I stay on

automatic.